Useful

Also by Peter Finch

The Peter Finch Archive is at
http://dialspace.dial.pipex.com/peter.finch/

Peter Finch
Useful

seren

seren
is the book imprint of
Poetry Wales Press Ltd
First Floor, 2 Wyndham Street
Bridgend, Wales

© Peter Finch 1997

Cataloguing In Publication Data for this title
is available from the British Library

ISBN 1-85411-176-0

*The publisher works with the financial support of the
Arts Council of Wales*

Cover: Polluted Pool at Maindee by Jack Crabtree
Courtesy of the National Museum and Gallery of Wales, Cardiff

Printed in Palatino by
The Cromwell Press, Melksham

Contents

Practice

Theory

Practice

The Versions

In one version the edges
were like Hokusai waves
and no one ever listened. In
another there was no periphery
just a vast spreading with
everything getting ever thinner.
In this one things bloom so
fast the hands go dizzy. Standing
in the back looking for coloured
stars, pushing the truth till
it talks, making the eyes do
everything. Flowers are suddenly
so significant   bent by
heat   like animals. You paint
these things by smoothing,
wiping, pressing, touching.   You
give them spirit   they
cease being   still so slowly.
Outside other versions wait
no one's looking.

Blonde Blues

The woman with the blonde hair talks to her son.
Her son is a great guitarist with a fine moustache.
His guitar is like a shooting star sometimes,
his hands full of driven chords and thrashing
blades of lights. She asks him if he is happy.
He is. Why does he move why does he play?
He must. Her hair cascades about her like a dance.
Sometimes she hears things which so deeply
move her she thinks she can make them herself
through sheer will. Here they are
like silver planes. She sighs.
She asks her son is it like this?
His fingers blur, his heart drips from
their tips. It is. She wonders if she can
roll the sky into a great crescendo of
notes. If she tries. He spins his arms
and does it for her. Blues like
a shower of rain. Inside she floats.

Talk About Nice Things

She has to be helped from the car now
muscles like knitted scarfs
her knees spread, wind wisps in her hair.
Her voice slips as vocabulary turns
to slush. She told me books
were too big. She liked talk
about nice things   nothing   how it was.
Her day shuffles dust, rearranges
antimacassars, grand rubber gloves.
When night falls television is
memory flickering on her walls.
She butters bread. The word for
love won't come, too distant. Sleep
stands like a dolmen in the hall.

Summer School

In the writer's class
the world has retired.
None of the students
fit the chairs.
Age has intervened.
    A woman with a chest
    like a coal sack sings
    cracked extracts from
    Gilbert and Sullivan. I am
    too polite to stop her.
They all seem to have
been coming here for
decades and no one
ever improves.
    We attempt a haiku
    for brevity. A dragon
    in a floral dress reads
    hers as if she were hailing
    a taxi. She is a thespian.
    The back row have
    misunderstood and supply sonnets.
    The man with the limp and
    the stained trousers talks about
    the war against the
    nip in Singapore.
I read Sylvester's
rendering of Basho,
best in the language
    Frog
    Pond
    Plop
ripple on ripple
a gulf away
from self-confession or
stuff about tramps.
    It is a matter of echoes
    I tell them.

A haiku suggests,
obliquely
is full of waves.
A harridan in the front row
puts her hand up.
Yes? Am I getting through?
Load of crap, she says.

Modernist

Once he put it down on paper he never changed it.
WW2 started in 1937, he wrote.
An easy mistake beaten by
Snowdon Scotland's highest peak then
Frank Bough, MP for Ynys Môn.
He went through life like it.
Early closing Friday, 50 bus to the docks,
Barry Island off the coast of Spain,
lost lorries asking him stayed lost.
It got worse as he got older.
Fish and cornflakes, paint-stripper vinegar,
Daz Ultra-Brite instead of toner in the copier.
Internal surrealism had him
parading through Debenhams' Spring Sale
in a bear skin singing,
lighting the frocks of shoppers with a zippo.
Old lady fireballs, toilets,
big dick drawings, importuning.
They locked him up.
Inside he found a fashion in perversity,
error was mutable, why not?
WW2 started in 1939 he eventually wrote
but by then it was too late.

Stones

all the stones possess are each other
edges worn by tide   underneath
are their souls   blue helmets
fists   paddle ends   tongues
they have causes, don't they?
pile at field edges
between the rotors
love the land.

I watch them gather in the bay
like an army   they could build
a wall, a harbour, couldn't they?
they don't

silent
like power sometimes,
you never know.
the shingle roars
it's a life.

Heart

warps of the heart
the unfulfilled heart
the bent heart

Late at night looking west when the Shirelles
come on the radio   the fridge clicking   the down
pipe loose   moon stars   like it has always been.

Sometimes the heart is so prominent that it
becomes a log wedged across the chest.

Does the heart have its own memory own
fears its own ghost way of talking
getting things done?

heart sways like a sabre
heart beats like a gong

In the morning rain running Lou Reed on
the Walkman chest a great house heart some
monster to be afraid of   I was in the weights
room sweat searing when my father died   my heart
engorged   his like a cold clam. How do you
breathe he'd asked me   afraid in the night
for the first time in 70 years   sink the shoulders
relax let it come   this technique
the only thing in a life I'd ever really given
him and in the end even this hadn't worked.

Sitting in the car park in the rain his
hat in a Tesco bag   trembling   heart moving
away from me faster   like an accelerating train.

The traces have smiles on them
smudges of voice   the imperfect
touch   all that remains.

Fists

When I form a fist
the index knuckle still stings
from the red mist a year ago when
I punched a hole in the wardrobe door.

We've exchanged hangers since.   Mine are
radio ariel diamonds.

Out the back are the boxes I won't
look in. Half a menu; sea shells;
kid's first shoe.

Time is in the next room, hissing like
a cistern. My fist is another fist now, of
course, the body renewed totally every
few years. Different bones, different
skin.

I pass you your junk mail. You put it
in your bin.

I walk behind people in crowds, imitating
their steps, not being me, seeing what it
is to be them.

It works occasionally, now and then. You
don't recognise me by the veg
in the supermarket.

My fist in the frozen peas. You with him.

The Writer on Holiday with Two Teenagers Sends a Postcard Home

Dear All,

You wouldn't like it here. Too much like the brochure, full of brightness and heat. Each day by eleven when the cloud has flaked westwards the sun is all we can see. We are at a cove, an artificially sanded rock inlet filled with the tideless med. This totteringly Spanish precursor to EuroDisney has been overrun by German car workers and is now one of the noisiest places on earth. Demonic children armed with giant crocodile beach rafts and submariner masks the size of televisions roar in circles. Housefrau like blistered sea-lions howl vociferously while their lobster husbands pay, what must be to them and their brilliant economy virtually nothing, to rent rust-blotched sombrillas and frayed tumbonas. Balearic heaven.

In the short time I have been here I have seen off Updike's *Rabbit*, Styron's *Sophie* and Keneally's *Ark*. My children have crouched in the shade gamely chasing the brothers Mario and manipulating screen-bound stacks of tetris blocks. I can discourse on the holocaust, on guilt and love and the place of god in this burning mess. They can move their fingers with a dexterity I'll never match. Culture changes. We drink cola stuffed with ice and slivers of lemon. I doze. With the love that only close family can show they berate each other for being alive.

It has been a week of angst, blame, teenage dissidence and untrammelled rage. Me burning in the swordfish sun attracting wasps of abuse like a melting sweet. You slap-headed queer shut up I'm telling you pay the bill you wanker don't make such a bloody fuss everyone looks why should bloody bugger bastard let me tosser you cock.

There are no clouds. Television is in Spanish. The bus to town is full.

Sometimes in small moments of respite arrived at by accident when the abuse softens into unwashed teenage sleep I reflect on how the great leaders of men must have skins like bunker concrete and ears as selective as Russian radio dials.

Sand in your suitcase, grit in your bedclothes, size nine green giant athletic footwear across your last fresh towel, suncream in your passport, your pen a blunt dart, your half-finished novel by Stan Barstow frisbeed out to sea at noon.

Virulence rises like steam as the med winks ever bluer in the slashing heat. On the horizon a white yacht grazes. Despite my tan I feel soft and bloodless. The Germans are buying everyone huge Minorcan frankfurters and splashing them with luminous mustard brought from home. I buy a three-day old Sunday newspaper for £5.50 and find the magazine, the arts supplement and the books section have all been jettisoned to save air weight. I swear a bit myself.

In the distance I can hear the hotel entertainer on loud hailer encouraging the Aryans by the pool to polka faster. The week smokes on like a three funnelled cruiser. I camouflage myself with Bronzotan. The beach is at least uncompromisingly topless. I adjust my dark glasses and permit a smile. Fucking homosexual shouts my son.

Best
P.

The Chicken of Depression

I had a dream last night
about chickens   you know how
it is   the memory slips so fast
like melting ice   I am in
the dining room   hating it   suddenly
these birds are friends with
names and memories   the microwave
stuffed solid with their ghosts

According to the psychology dreaming
of poultry underlines perversity.
The bluebird of happiness long absent
from his life, Ned is visited by the
chicken of depression. I'm Ned.
Line on a Christmas card sent by a
well-wisher. In the fourteenth
century they thought the soul was
a sac near the pancreas about the
size of a small pullet.
I can feel mine pecking
mouth of feathers, neck of fire.

In the dream the sky closed
over with a million hens flying
chicken darkness   no moon

Birds don't have souls you know
they circle endlessly
hoping for forgiveness

it's safe in heaven.

The Steps

In front of the museum
too expensive now for Cardiffians
where John Tripp hid
his bicycle clips among the pillars
and the statue of Lloyd George
greens slowly in the drizzle
I saw Tom Jones once
eluding fans among the bushes.

Heart of the Welsh universe
its white portland replicated
perfectly in India
where the architect made a quick
rupee reselling his plans.

The past concentrates on these slabs.
Memory of marches, meetings, passions,
hired coaches like cream river-boats
the steps cut like a ghat on the Ganges.
When the sea rises
the tide will reach here with ease.

Lambies

The Wentloog Levels between Cardiff and Newport

Climb up, you can do it. Top of the sea wall
overgrown with fox tail, bent grass, cranesbill,
ribwort, speedwell. The fields here flat, crossed
with reans foreign as Mars taking the swamp away.
We walk single file. Shelduck on the
mudflats, groyne teeth, breakwater, boat-ribs,
wrecked hard-core, the slope to the sea estuary
toughened with a boulder skin rough as navigator's
hands.

The ponds they've built for fish look real enough,
ditch and slack joined behind the Peterstone Sluice,
but up close their Disney geography belies the buckling
winds, neat angling piers made of log, clips
for catchnets, fences. The sea-board warning sign
rain eroded. Do Not. The path thickens with
heavy cock's-foot. As if we would.

The flats stretch away into sunlight alive with
thunder-cloud, waste mud like thrown paint. Cars
are smashed here, brick, city detritus, logs
drifted with scoured plastic, cans. Blue smoke off the
last beaches, gravel, waste concrete, sand.

Across the Channel the Somerset Levels as wrecked
as these. Distant hammering as some kid smashes
a bus shelter and the thug-roar of a high-cleated
Kawasaki carving across grass. Behind us chicaned,
traffic-calmed housing merges slowly with wilderness.
Gull overhead in a turning cloud. Soon they're gone.

Cars

they used to mend cars in our street
all of them   shammying headlamps
draining sumps   fat terry with a
jaguar walnut leather spanners
engine parts laid out on the pavement like art
mr brown thirteen years exorcising rust
from a faded citroen   the manzarettis
faking speed bolting chrome
onto family saloons   gone

in the new world   this one
where the heart is invisible   the
pavements are solid with white skirted
coupes shining they start everytime

I park in the next street run to work
I am always running   the next task is
always more important than this one   arrive
as fast as I can   I know
none of the owners   coats   hats   important
things on their faces   mine is empty
or inscrutable   standing on the front
path with a foam-loaded car brush
wondering breathlessly where now   the
family no longer live here   clean spaces   ghosts

couldn't make it go   yesterday   rain   terry
would have given me a lift   the bus
runs from somewhere I've never been before

are we rich   my son asks me I tell him no   no
not yet.

All I Need is Three Plums

apologies to William Carlos Williams

I have sold your jewellery collection,
which you kept in a box, forgive me.
I am sorry, but it came upon me
and the money was so inviting, so sweet
and so cold.

I have failed to increase my chest measurements
despite bar bells
and my t-shirt is not full of ripples.
I am sweet but that is no consolation.
You hand is cold.

I did not get the job, your brother did.
He is a bastard I told him, forgive me.
The world is full of wankers, my sweet.

I have lost the dog, I am sorry.
He never liked me, I am hardly inviting.
I took him off the lead in the park and
the swine chased a cat I couldn't
be bothered to run after him.
Forgive me, I will fail less in the
future.

I have collected all the furniture I could find
and dismembered it in the grate, I am sorry,
but I have these aberrations.
The weather is inclement. You have run out of
firelighters.
It's bloody cold.

Please forgive me, I have taken the money
you have been saving in the ceramic pig
and spent it on drink, so sweet and inviting.
This is just to say I am in the pub
where I have purchased the fat guy from

Merthyr's entire collection of scratch and win.
All I need now is three delicious plums.

Forgive me, sweetie,
these things just happen.

The Future

In my rainy first year the slates were large
and patterned with scribble. We sat in
circles hands full of plasticine. No one
wrote a thing. The walls were massed
with daubs of colour. Painting.

After summer we moved into rows and drew
firm lines on sheets of sugar paper. Miss
Evans applauded our precision although
mine was like the sea. By Christmas it
had calmed into archipelagoes. She said
I was a late starter. What did we need
to write for? There was a universe on
radio.

In form four I practised my signature
into an illegible calligraph. Like
Picasso. It worked on Postal Orders.

Before I moved schools, at eleven, they
told my mother to encourage me away
from comics. She bought a television.

If you can be like that she exclaimed
pointing at Albert Tatlock and his
Northern cohorts, you'll make a
fortune.

Too many books make you weak. In
the real world there are only fists
and money.

Eventually one great day we had
certificates saying how good we were.
So much for thinking, for arguing, for
getting it right. Writing wasn't
mentioned.

The future is yours, said the head, glad
to have got rid of it. The world outside
didn't alter but we went to look. Still
raining.

Useful

I ave bought Carl an ackers kit
book an a disk
with it he says he can talk
to some arsehole in the Pentagon
set off bombs on ships
lots of typing bloody brilliant
stops im nickin cars it does
an setting fire to animals.

Shirts

My shirts are a history. A cupboard full
of decades strung worn-shouldered on grey wire.
There are ticket stubs in some pockets.
The Beatles At The Cardiff Capitol. Left there
like a mummy fragment and with just the
same power. In the cuffs are dust from
old affairs; a scuff of lipstick along a
white sleeve; ghosts of energy and purpose
I could never revive now. I show these
to my son who thinks of the past as one
long carnival. Polka shirts for dancing,
purple decades of unrelieved lust.
He cannot yet place pain in the precedence
of emotions. The biggest thing in the
world is still no tie and a ripple of
silk on a Saturday. It's the best way to be.

Meeting Her Lover

I cannot talk to him about football
because I don't know enough. The game
roars on the television like a floundering
ship. I try books but he doesn't respond.
With his fat eyes he looks so dumb.
We try weather it's as exciting as
tyre pressures and motorway routes.
Outside the sun is enormous.
His car is shit fast he tells me I
couldn't give a damn. On the
screen the goals mount like fever,
men embracing on the green sward.
You take her then, I say, as
if this woman is still something I
have a hold on. But he's not looking,
the game's being played again,
on and on.

Takes Guts

I thought all this would be okay
getting arseholed lunchbreak then going
back on the job and pretending I was
okay enough to work the sheet press.
You know the form: stand around pull
the lever piece of piss so long as you
don't fall in. As it was we'd put
Morgans' lunchbox through the
quarter-inch mill and stood it
like a Tom and Jerry thing in his
locker, bits of four-foot tomato
sandwich and pressed tin. Mickey had
filled the guy's bike frame with
industrial mercury. When he tried to
get it out of the rack he'd think his
arms had failed. The whole afternoon
was like this, paint fights and helium
gargling. A fucking hoot until I got
my coverall caught under the cutter
and since the travel-stop had unscrewed
lost a slice of gut. Through the pethidine
fog I can hear Morgans telling me
self-inflicteds don't count for benefit
and that I was too fat anyway. Wanker.
Wait until he gets to remilling the failed
castings. His bucket has been wired direct
into the 240. No one's gone that far
before. Takes guts.

De Kooning at the Three Brewers

He is Willem de Kooning
striding down Melrose Avenue.

You can tell from his paint-stained hands,
his baseball hat, his American gait.

His works are huge, incoherent face-offs
between will and fate.

He moves his arms
the drinkers recognise his Alzheimer's genius.

The shapes he makes are
hips and bulging thighs.

Inside he is wherever his spirit leads him
not here among the lager debris.

The fitters are
slick wet colour.

The dart players are
lucid curves.

The azure sky lies
on the chrome yellow car-park.

The smokers' shrill reds
dot the vastness of their dreams.

His sight is empty
the typists swirl in molten sprays.

Nothing cuts now like it did.
At the bar the drinkers nod their heads.

Sick

There are lots of things wrong with me,
some of them recently discovered,
others been around for an age and
only now worry me enough to complain.
They are rolling about and I must take
action. I have seen the doctor he
says try being black like him
and see how I get on. Writes me a
script for white pills. I throw it
in the hedge. These are dark days.
I guess it's okay to say that.

I have hot-dog headaches, sexual dysfunction,
melancholia, impetigo, somnambulant shin splints,
bruxism and improper bite, draconionisis,
jack sprat and wife syndrome, turkish molluscs,
constitutional blahs, turtle sunstroke and
rodent bones. It's a powerful list.

You wonder how I walk if it's that bad.
Some of us have no option.
Listen to me, you rich bastard,
give me love, peace and happiness
and it will certainly stop.

The Meeting

These guys have piercing blue
eyes like cerulean light pulls. In
the huge room they cluster
the table for fear of cold corners
and tell us we've been
sold to someone else. You can
hear your own breath when
you get news like that.

I could have done with some caffeine
but none was offered   back of my
throat like a dried shoe liner
and the big speech   you know
fuck off you bastards   that one
it wouldn't come up out of anywhere.

I could feel my whole skeleton
strung by hope and hard grit
coming apart inside my clothes.
Click in the vent system   slow
hum   better noise than
anything else around.

They helped me on with my mack as
I left.   Never done that before.

All She Says

Down the end of the telephone line she's still there imagining that she's got the world right. Her voice has shifted after all these years. Rougher, the words have less grace, but it's still her. She loves this new guy. She doesn't say anything now about how real it is, how different, how much better. But you can tell by the way she sticks, stays there. She wants to borrow the mower and wouldn't have dreamt to ask before knowing you'd have to bring it, trailing dried grass, mud and grit, out through the hallway and across the front path. She says the kids are fine. Did you get the birthday card Jamie sent? He made it himself. You want to get the conversation round to could we manage it again now. After all this time we're new people, we've learned a million things about how the world actually works and just how we are inside it. You wonder for a minute what you'd do if she said yes. But it's no problem, she's interrupted by her door bell, nothing changes, she has to go.

"You know we should meet, you know. Maybe we could do that?" You get that out at least, blustering, nervous, but the phone silence all around is immense.

"Look, bring the mower round. I'd appreciate it. I've got to go."
That's all she says.

Stone Clasps

The leaf won't lift with the broom, frost laced, frozen to the quarry-tiled path. My father laid this out, told me how, appraised the door architrave, complained about the bare hall floor. I fixed it. He's gone.

This house is at the flux of three churches, one at each street end, another two roads off, length of a football field if you could stand high enough to shout. While my father lived, arriving in his gleaming cars, these stone clasps of god stayed invisible. Feast days they'd flush and shimmer but their own fathers stayed deep inside them, full of the past.

I bend down and breathe warmth on the palmate lobes, unglue them with my own vital force. Three years since his voice echoed anywhere around here yet when I need to hear it it's still there. I see the priests and pastors now walking to their sanctuaries. I recognise them by their steady gait, I know who they are. Their bodies are upright like antennae, they carry small packages in their arms. Their churches are half empty but remain such strong places. I have gone to them and leant my hands to feel the spirit in their walls. Death can make you need. The chinks in your armour blink and at night, inexplicably, you fear.

The leaf comes free to leave a damp mark its own shape, a ghost. My father walks on between the churches. I see them waiting with their ancient faces. I look but that's all I do. I go in and replace the broom. It's much too soon.

Marks

The path is light brick, level, gaps unmortared, most of the surfaces mossing slowly. The world is everything outside his skin. This day the wind blows through it but there is no rain.

He makes things, usually. Shifts ideas into new places, looks at them from different angles. Occasionally they give off light. When he sees a shape he likes he writes it down.

Does this act change anything? The moon pulls the sea up, bathes the degenerate path with a light the moss hardly feels. He is afraid at times that his mark will not outlive him. And in this damp climate where ink runs murky like the memories which recall it why should anything stay?

His notebooks make a fine stack in the long room. He watches the sky for new light wondering if the gloom goes on forever now. Then, unaccountably, it happens again. Inside. Outside. Who knows.

The River

We travel. The new road runs high up over the estuary. You can watch the river touch the sea here. The blending of waters, not river, not sea; a rolling, two shaded place of suck and swirl. My companion talks of white-water rafting in Alaska and the excitement of free-falling 100 meters through churning rock, alone. But I'm only half listening. This river — Welsh, dirty, slow — ends like it began, like the Welsh do most things — not exactly, not precisely, in no single place, in no markable spot, no trigonometrical point, no reference, no marker, no writ, no underlined thrice signboard, but it does end. The river stops, amorphously, somewhere out there, in the blue-grey mesh of the spinning world.

I hunted its source once amid the highest hills we have, hummocks, really, barely reaching 3000 feet but wild enough. Up there, crossing ridge on ridge, expecting a bubbling I could put my fist to I discovered instead a thousand sources, a great seeping, no one point I could mark with my boot heel. A meandering, a wonderful vagueness, like the sky, like the sea itself, like the void.

My companion tells me most countries have rivers bigger than this one. I tell her that doesn't matter at all.

Theory

Walking

Bob Cobbing Dances – Still Doing It

Self-Portrait

Anglo-Welsh Studies

RNLD TOMOS (*vcl, hca*) aka Curtis Langdon. Born 1913. Gospel. Austerity tradition. Jnd Iago Prytherch Big Band (1959), notch, crack, gog, gap, bwlch, tan, iaith, mynydd, adwy — mainly on Hart-Davis race label. Concert at Sherman support Sorley Maclean (*gtr, hrt clutching*) sold out. A pioneer of dark wounds and internal tensions. To live in Wales is to become un-assailable. "An angel-fish" (Clarke). Still recording.

Partisan

rydw i am fod blydi I am
rydyn ni rydw i rody i
rodney rodney I am
rydyn am fod I am I am I am
rydw i yn Pantycelyn Rhydcymerau Pwllheli yes

I am bicupping mainly cym sticker ardvark
the dictionary cymro hirsuit weirdo
on fire arrested finger-pointed rydych chi
imperialist long-nosed pinky cottagers

roeddwn i'n fine yn y bore oherwydd
y heddlu not able anyway little zippo
lager considerable influence
tried to burn it not enough alcoalcohol
corner shop four-pack Diamond White Red Stripe
brns your heart out

rudin wedi dysgu hen ddigon ol' mouldering
Welsh Saunders Mabinignog crap
nasty blydi books   we're a video neishyn
smot superbod sam tan brilliant exampl

ac yn nawr?
bod ar y satellite no defense
carchar poms yn saesneg
dim yn gallu handlo'r cymraeg
rîl traditional blydi welshman.

How the Blues Work

You get a hit on Aladdin Records, West Coast R and B label. You have a voice that has a hollowness that makes it sound almost like an echo of itself.

The waitresses react very strongly to this resorting to such tactics as the use of freak high notes, the relentless honking on a single beat for an entire chorus, the use of honking instead of menus with the patrons certainly taking to this gimme dat thing down there wid the shaking bits and the use of low notes with deliberately vulgar tonal effects.

If the blues is trouble music then the country bluesmen get this by wailing and the urban bluesmen by analysis. So many honkers struggling to entertain half-baked labourers on battered uprights and wrecking their voices on inadequate amplifiers.

You may smile at all this being depressed and singing about it, putting your head on the railway line before the train comes, gonna do a little boogie-woogie here. How do you put emotional sincerity into these things? Jack the baseball hat, wear wide lapels.

Best blues singers seem like battle cruisers. So big. Their mouths can kiss and could hum Mozart. Really they could. But they don't.

The Vacuum Warriors Get Free Tickets

Warriors went to Catraeth   with the Hoover
with the dawn   with the day   with the eager
laughter

Warriors wearing a brooch   a meal-nourished host
a boisterous youth   a hydrovac   an optional
extra crevice tool

they stain three javelins
three fierce kings   three battle-peers

rising early on castors
the blood flowing   crimson garments
indestructible rompers

they are effortless
these cleaning pads
these warriors suck

accessories include:
woe   grief   generosity
swiftness   sharp spears
the Son of Tegfan
and an additional chrome handle

Warriors went to Catraeth   hunting for money
the wall of battle   Hoover coupons
the earth now covers the Hoover offer
injury, and no advantage, did they receive

Poetry is now parted from the airliner

The Way it Grows

on mud and in shallow water
confined to gardens
in crevices on slopes
on waste ground and waste places
and waste woodland on hedgebanks
in shingle on sand in shaded limestone
and damp grassland near streams on
thin soils and salt-marshes
on dry grasslands and bogs and coastal
cliffs in walls on the banks of ditches
on rubbish tips and sand dunes and
wet cliff ledges and rocky places
and thickets in woodland on riverbanks
and damp scrub and high ground and
shallow soils on grassy heaths and hill
slopes and marshy pools and salt-marshes
and cornfields on flushes in low fore-dunes
and muddy creeks and estuaries and marshy
driftlines on dune slacks and muddy
edges in conifer plantation and beech-woods
and grasslands behind spoil-tips on marsh edges
and waste field banks and headlands
in brackish ditches and sown
roadsides on spray zones and
water reaches and acid tongues
on marshes under hedges on strewn-floors
in distrusting argument and outmoded
pairings in damp boredom on child-trodden
guilt and urban crap dumps under piecemeal
thickets of antipathy, alcohol and despair in
marshy foreshores of misogynist sex and
tears and rage and endless duplicity
in the spray of other things and other strains
and other lusts and other needs.
When it doesn't feel right you throw it.
When it doesn't work you don't fix it you
dump it jesus when it ceases to flower
you mash it and in the mess of bog
and marsh inside you oh how it streams
oh how it leers

The Exhibition

Man With Towel Drying His Tongue
oil on canvas 30" x 20"

Bright Nude With Crown
pastel on paper 10" x 16"

Self-Portrait With Star On Stick
mixed-media 40" x 60"

Triptych - Nudes Embracing, Nudes Struggling, Nudes Parting
oil on paper with felt roofing strips 30" x 8 yards

Self-Portait With Stick And Ripped Shirt
pencil 2" x 2"

Portrait Of The Artist As A Misogynist,
tongue between teeth
oil on canvas with eyeliner applique and
glued beer cans,
collection G. Broding

Views From Inside The Wardrobe
mixed-media — tin bath, water and electric kettle element

This Is How It Is Now
instamatic assemblage of artist looking miserable
in various parts of the city 40" x 30"
collection R. Knowles, private investigator

Untitled
body tattoo "I Love You" crossed out with blue biro
NFS

Small Man With Bottles
charcoal on burned paper 10" x 10"
collection the artist.
print available, enquire at desk

Dark curtain for obscuring door.

Stuck

QUICK BROWN FOX QWERTY
this user's mouse dropped in the
butter   pink-smear on screen
from nail varnish   'A' sticks
from bashing   lost temper when
file crshed   cnt unslot floppy
drive full of fg ush   printer
out of ink   spryed ribbon with
WD40 top tip Cyber Bodger's Monthly
slime on roller   sod blck hnds
@#*}&%%<>M%o)   unplug

Sonnet No. 18

Eeeee e eeeeeee eeee ee e eeeeee's eee?
Eeee eee eeee eeeeee eee eeee eeeeeeooo:
Ooooo ooooo oo ooooo ooo ooooooo oooo oo Ooo,
Ooo oossss's sssss ssss sss sss sssss s ssss:
Ssssssss sst ttt ttt ttt tt tttttt tttttt,
Ttt ttttt tt ttt ttta aaaaaaaaaa aaaa'a:
Aaa aaaaa aaaa aaaa aaaa aaannnnn nnnnnnnn,
Nn nnnnnn, nn nnnnnn'n hhhhhhhhh hhhhhh hhhhhhh'h;
Hhh hh hrrrrrr rrrrrr rrrrr rrr rrrr,
Rrr rrri iiiiiiiiii ii iiii iiii iill ll'll,
Lll lllll lllll llll lllm mmmmmm'mm mm mmm mmmmm,
Mmmd dd dddddddd ddddd dd dddu uuuu uuuu'uu;
  Uu uuff ff fff fff ffggggg, gg gggg ggc ccc,
  Cc cccc ccyyy yyyy, www wwwv vvvvb bbbb pp ppkx.

52

Meeting New People

Stress bends the accent. The list an unchecked
check list stress recheck. I mispronounce
Body, Polley, Dworkin, Malin, Misanthropy,
Diatribe, Arbitrary, Body Rub, Weather Front.
Look across the gulf, filled with conditioned air.
Tick note.

Your name is Andrea. Your name is Andrea.
Your name is Andrea. Your name is Angela.

Tag unreadable. Most of this exists through
e-mail. 10:45 am the system is down. 10:51 am
system repaired. 11:05 system undone again.

Angela explains the world as cloud cumulus
strata herringbone on a ticked list.

Ask at reception. Free use. Glass vase of
business cards. They call me Mr French.
They don't know. They shake my hand.

Wet Singers

Water Jones
Blind Wet Jenkins
Bog Stitchwort Owen
The Waterstones
Foam Baby
West Glamorgan Pipe Choral
Crow Edward Rainfall
Damp Diddley Davies
The Shower Kings Oh Such Piping Hot Harmony
Tin Bath Malcolm (gtr)
The Physicians of Myddfai
Thomas The Tank Engine

One of Our Presidents:
Six Variations
for Tony Conran

mark Conran toiler
eye bright eye old one opposite
no fish noxiousness too far inland
hook jetty over miserable history

so courteous camel eyes this man
eyes other all eyes the ones
fish leap the neat silver
riotous head who'd know they do
ox-eye, amorous, ending endless
fish our waters, hunt the new

one

old one opposite no fish noxiousness too far
inland hook jetty over miserable history so courteou
s camel eyed this man eyes other all eye

ones fish leap the neat leap the neat endl
our waters, hunt the ran toiler
bright eye old one opposite
no fish noxious
ness inland leap the neat silver
our waters, our waters,
our waters, our waters.

two

one eyed amorous endling endless
hook toiler bright old oppos
light jetty miserable neat
fish leap the fish leap the
all eyes the waters

eye bright eye old one opposite
noxiousness too far inlan
hook jet eyed this man
who'd know they do ox-eye
amorous, ending mark endless

three

the toiler
mark toiler
bright eyed old toil
inland for toiling

miserable courteous neat silver
all eyes the ones fish leap
they do ox-eye toiling
hunt toiling bright toiler
mark Conran this man
bright leaping all silver

four

mk con toiler bright
neat silver riot
us amorous ish usness
inland is nes ish rous

ish aters is man silver
endless is less endless
camel eye neat who'd know
osite rable mistory Conran
leap con who'd know us is ending
our less sliv neat eye ox endless

five

mark bright fish anxiousness
miserable miserable miserable
miserable miserable miserable
miserable who'd know

ending bright ending all eyes the ones
Conran no ending our ending
ding less amorous opposite who'd leap
hunt the neat the ones the silver
so courteous bright anxiousness
riotous camels who know the silver

six

A note on the compositional methods used for
"One of our Presidents".

In an alphabet identified by the poet Jackon Mac Low
(Sandra Lawrence's "The Roman Inscriptional Letter") and
again in the anonymous Middle-English poem "Aristotle's
ABC" letters are given specific meanings. A=ox, B=house,
C=camel, and so on under Lawrence and A=amorous, B=
bold, C=courteous, etc., under Aristotle. To originate my
text I allocated meanings forming the name Tony Conran,
one set to each line. Line one, T for Tony, for example,
gave me both "toilous" and "mark". Line two, O, gave me
"eye", "opposite" and "other". Once written the piece was
extended and varied using a structural process devised
from Conran's poem "Blodeuwedd". The number of letters
in each line of this poem were used as a process guide to
my own text, with punctuation and spaces acting as
direction and repeat indicators. The piece stops here at
variation six although there is still plenty of fire left and
one day I will carry it on.

Things That Can Go Wrong for Painters

Small punctures of oiliness, failed surface regeneration, misuse of knives, weakened slits in the soul, growth of green penicillium, varnished bloom, fine lines in the rigging of ships, cloud scumbles, glazed foilage in the grip of mornings, hard mouths, weak stippling, weak rinsing, weak method, weak edge, cheap wood-pulp, weak new linen, weak cut and strap, slit and re-stretched taut, flat face of the painting and its weakened line, application of water with care avoiding the checkerboard effect and the dust of which cities are never free and the sunsets and the dark and the endless desire, cutting away the paper for lining and repairing with toxic chemicals. Ethylene heart stretched and steamed, aching, aching, cracked and cupped. The head is an unyeilding concavity which emphasizes its crushed condition. Love sticks to almost every material except silicone. Touch and remain. Hold and sway. For years there will be unmistakable evidence of pressure, the crackle, the ir-regularities, the unequal tension and the smouldering fire, the aching arms, the eyes which do not sleep, the timelessness of the heart, the way it never ends.

What to do:

The antidote is to tear, slice, obscure, apply paint by dripping, partially paste then tear away, burn and scorch, strip away, splash or splatter paint then tear away, float colour on water then transfer then tear, crumple, rub, crumble, rub, texture, rub, then tear, smoke, burn, rub, scratch, rub, scrape, rub, stick, find, unstick, rub, batter, find battered, cut and rub, splatter and rub, roll and rub, rip and splatter, unglue, restrip, rub, split, hoe, scrape, seed, water, rag-glue, rub, remove rub reglue rip retear rip rub unglue reglue peel smear bend balk stipple drop rip resplatter sniff uncover display cut underline rub layer undo redo remix unmix uncover rerub redo rub rerub unrub prerub rerub. It lasts for a while. This fragile surface. Then you start again.

The Hancock Furniture Poem

Cupboards are life
  I am a sideboard

The world is full of gate legs
    bevelled bookshelves
glass-backed corner things
    mahogany knitting holders
and elaborately quilted sponge-free
    bidet armchairs
                    mate

  yes

furniture

furniture
  is such sweet sorrow

I am purple
  you are laminated

plink plonk plank

Places

(Bannau Brycheiniog, The Brecon Beacons)

the bridge of stile
the folding hill
the rock of the black peak
the dock leaf meadow
the perfect crest of the perfect crest
the perfect meadow
the cold valley
the meadow of streams
the rocks of the place of pools
the little back dear back
the perfect peak
the white hollow
the mound in the street of nooks
the stream of bells
the valley of cotton grass
the ridge of stone
the slope of sheep
the roaring crest
the path of feet
the perfect boot
the pathless waste
the cold place
the withering cleats
the bee of bikes
the brown distress
the friable edge
the mist the rain the perfect rain
the astroturf
the macadamed ridge
the push chair access
the wimpey site
not yet not yet
but soon

Cutting Up

Burroughs said they were all unable grey
rope veins semen jacked off loose flaps
like bits of offal sliding stained plastic
bronchial mucous no passion but all of them
reading culture thick with resonance
nothing to stop anyone quoting Aristophanes
bundling their visions into yellow envelopes
smacking their famous arms wobbly and
sliding the needle in.

The history of this makes it okay. We're
forearmed and safe with an army of pioneers
told the consequences all written up
but no one reads that jack shit.

Out there now most of them biker jacketed without
bikes £60 Taiwan impossibly genuine manipulating
slick lager cans never riding any boxcar
except the bus which won't run late now after
the driver took a Groche in the nose.

Culture is de-cultured the redeeming poetry of
suede boots dossing with a mouth of Rimbaud gone
the same way as most of the other little freedoms
replaced by pig everything garbage polystyrene
sliced nipples strung dicks ornamented fuck off
forehead tattooed in 72-point Times Roman which
retired at sixty will spice-up the booze queue
at Asda or maybe not.

Most of the team leaders you could blame for
it are dead Parker Kerouac Jim Morrison Ginsberg like
a bank clerk. Put your hand up if you recognise
these rebels inflammatory bastards Brossard
Solomon Trocchi Krim Bremser Orlovsky you are too
old all of you doesn't count. God even Larkin

when he couldn't make it to the bogs pissed in his overcoat. Do it again not progress rites of passage cut up the cut-up cut-up reinvented cut-up repeats.

Truth

I am having trouble with the
truth when I started out the truth
I had a mission truth is I believed
truth a passion but the zealous
relax fingers tarnish I am on a bus
not often now but this time
a parent speaking imperfectly to a downs child
trees at high speed   tone smiling heart full
iaith so fractured child can't manage   bachgen
bach bugger all we do is stick up the
culture with blutak truth too
irrelevant   child smiles amid
a pat of anifeilaidd mutter
iaith y nefoedd never ours or
our fault ever got off
she tried that woman by her
own lights truth's a bastard.

Written Out

There are five types of evil which come on
       us when we stop trying.
First is the formation of alliances
       to denigrate the wise works of others
       you recognise these
Second is the way we luxuriate in new editions
       old songs like shiny beasts
       commas retreaded
Third is an oppressive interest in charms, fate,
       it'll be alright on the night
       my puddings always rise God ordained it
Fourth is judgement based on hearsay
       read nothing for twenty years
       nothing reported
Fifth is lining up others like ourselves
       into cabals of aged malfunction
       little more to say
       bar abrogation.
       There is nothing new under the sun
       and the sun is sinking.

It is all treacherous and immoral and
       you should distance yourself

Until of course it becomes inevitable.

Like an Uncle

The age I get to is amazing.
I listen closely and hear the
past moving away like buffalo across the plains.
The hooves still speak.
It's a fun time, they tell me,
the kids leaving, all the adjustments bolted,
the patterns screwed tight down
and people getting famous, big famous,
so famous they can't breathe
glowing   thick like velvet curtains
it happens   blazing fame the air full of motes.
This fame you remember, don't you?
Famous so bloody famous
so easy   history of smiling,
hats, my collection of china dogs,
the six mile nose, juggling,
a bottle of sherry in a raffle once
can you imagine
just like an uncle.

Notes

"The Versions": a poem which is as much about painting as it is about relationships. Illustrated and produced as a limited edition print by the artist William Brown.

"Summer School": Sylvester is Dom Sylvester Houedard (1924-1992), the Benedictine monk and concrete poet from Prinknash Abbey famed for his minimalist rendering of Matsuo Basho's (1644-1694) most celebrated haiku.

"All I Need is Three Plums": I am not the first to use William Carlos Williams' note to his wife "This is Just to Say" as a starting point for humorous verse making. Kenneth Koch has done so, as have others. Mine celebrates the fruit machine scratch & win charity card which was sold by the thousands in pubs up and down the country before the advent of Camelot's National Lottery.

"The Meeting": The management buy-out of the Oriel Bookshop in Cardiff failed. The Arts Council of Wales transferred the whole operation to HMSO in April, 1995.

"The River": My companion was the American public artist, Mags Harries, with whom I worked on the 1995 Swansea Year of Literature Tŷ Llen Demons Project. The river is the Neath.

"Walking"(for Eric Mottram): Eric was a great walker and although I never accompanied him we often talked about places we both had visited. This tribute, produced while he was still alive, was made by photocopying his entire *Selected Poems* (North & South, 1989) onto a single sheet then re-arranging this by rip, fold and tear. The coloured dot, Mottram lost in the rains of the Welsh countryside, recalls Marcell Duchamp's similarly dotted ready-made "Pharmacy".

"Bob Cobbing Dances — Still Doing It" was made for the Cobbing 75th birthday supplement to *And* magazine edited by Adrian Clarke. The letter forms originate from the Swansea Demon project, dry cleaning fluid makes them blur.

"Self-Portrait" 12"x8", letraset and acrylic, was commisioned for the Intimate Portraits Exhibition at the Glyn Vivian Gallery, Swansea in 1995.

"Anglo-Welsh Studies": a page from the 1989 Carcanet edition of Caradoc Evans's *Nothing To Pay* containing a paper blemish suggested further working.

"RNLD TOMOS": Thomas's pseudonym in his school magazine was Curtis Langdon. Hart-Davis published his early works.

"How the Blues Work": sourced (and considerably re-worked) from Arnold Shaw's *Honkers and Shouters − The Golden Years of Rhythm & Blues* (Collier Books, 1978).

"The Vacuum Warriors Get Free Tickets": a traditional cut-up from A.O.H. Jarman's edition of Aneirin's "Gododdin" and a Hoover catalogue.

"The Way it Grows": a process piece derived in part from *The Natural History Museum: Flora of Glamorgan* by A.E. Wade, Q.O. Kay and R.G. Ellis (HMSO, 1994).

"Sonnet No. 18": composed for a special issue of Glyn Pursglove's *The Swansea Review*. The piece reduced Shakespeare's most famous sonnet to its component letters restructured to mirror the form of the original work.

"Things That Can Go Wrong for Painters": sourced and processed from Ralph Mayer's *The Artists' Handbook of Materials & Techniques* (Faber, 1951).

"The Hancock Furniture Poem": the cue for this piece was "The Poetry Society" episode of Hancock's Half-Hour, first broadcast in 1959. Tejo Remy, the Dutch avant-garde furniture maker, built a strap-on, wooden poem box which the poet wore while reading. My performance, premiering this poem, took place in Remy's exhibition at the Oriel Gallery in 1994.

Acknowledgements

Some of the pieces in this collection have previously appeared in:

Ambit, And, Acumen, Blue Cage, Envoi, Fire, Intimate Portraits (Seren), *Malahat Review* (Canada), *Mesechabe Review* (USA), *Navis, New Welsh Review, News That Stays News, Object Permanence, Odyssey, Planet, Poetry Wales, The Rialto, Spear, Spokes, Staple, Swansea Review, Tears in the Fence, The Third Day* edited by Kathy Miles (Gomer), *The Urgency of Identity* edited by David Lloyd (TriQuarterly Books, USA), *West Coast Magazine, Wide Skirt, Yellow Crane, The Visual Word* exhibition catalogue edited by Keith Bayliss (Swansea Arts Workshop — Cardiff Old Library).

"Stones" is the text for a limited edition print made with the artist William Brown.

"Useful" and "Stuck" were commissioned pieces for the Teliesyn television production *Cyber Wales*.

"Walking" was a commission for the Eric Mottram tribute anthology *Alive In Parts Of This Century* edited by Peterjon and Yasmin Skelt and published by North and South.

"RNLD TOMOS" was written as part of a poem-poster collaboration with the artist Paul Peter Piech.

"One of Our Presidents: Six Variations for Tony Conran" was written for the Welsh Union of Writers' tribute anthology *Shaman of Shifting Form*, edited by Nigel Jenkins.